FIRST SCIENCE

Magnetism

by Mari Schuh

BLASTOFF! READERS 4

BELLWETHER MEDIA • MINNEAPOLIS, MN

Note to Librarians, Teachers, and Parents:

Blastoff! Readers are carefully developed by literacy experts and combine standards-based content with developmentally-appropriate text.

Level 1 provides the most support through repetition of high-frequency words, light text, predictable sentence patterns, and strong visual support.

Level 2 offers early readers a bit more challenge through varied simple sentences, increased text load, and less repetition of high frequency words.

Level 3 advances early-fluent readers toward fluency through increased text and concept load, less reliance on visuals, longer sentences, and more literary language.

Level 4 builds reading stamina by providing more text per page, increased use of punctuation, greater variation in sentence patterns, and increasingly challenging vocabulary.

Level 5 encourages children to move from "learning to read" to "reading to learn" by providing even more text, varied writing styles, and less familiar topics.

Whichever book is right for your reader, Blastoff! Readers are the perfect books to build confidence and encourage a love of reading that will last a lifetime!

This edition first published in 2011 by Bellwether Media, Inc.

No part of this publication may be reproduced in whole or in part without written permission of the publisher. For information regarding permission, write to Bellwether Media, Inc., Attention: Permissions Department, 5357 Penn Avenue South, Minneapolis, MN 55419.

Library of Congress Cataloging-in-Publication Data
Schuh, Mari C., 1975–
  Magnetism / by Mari Schuh.
    p. cm. – (Blastoff! readers) (First science)
Summary: "First Science explains introductory physical science concepts about magnetism through real-world observation and simple scientific diagrams. Intended for students grades three through six"–Provided by publisher.
  Includes bibliographical references and index.
  ISBN 978-0-531-28456-8 (paperback : alk. paper)
  1. Magnetism–Juvenile literature. 2. Magnets–Juvenile literature. I. Title.
  QC753.7.S38 2008
  538–dc22   2007010298

Printed in the United States of America.   010111   1185

Contents

Magnets   4

What Is Magnetism?   6

Magnetic Poles   12

Magnetic Earth   16

Magnets in Use   20

To Learn More   22

Glossary   23

Index   24

Magnets

Have you ever stuck a magnet to your refrigerator?

Maybe you've played with toy magnets. Do you know why magnets work like they do?

What Is Magnetism?

A magnet has an invisible force called magnetism. Magnetism makes magnets stick to other magnets or metals, such as **iron** and **steel**. Metals that stick to magnets are called **magnetic** metals.

Most refrigerator doors are made of steel. Paper clips are also made of steel. Look how well they stick to a magnet. What other objects around you might stick to a magnet?

The force of magnetism doesn't work on all metals. Try holding a magnet to a **copper** penny or an **aluminum** can. You will see it doesn't work. Copper and aluminum are not magnetic.

If you move a magnet slowly toward a steel ball, the ball will roll toward the magnet and jump to it. Magnets pull on metals even before they touch them. The pull gets stronger the closer the magnet gets to the metal. This pulling force is also magnetism.

Magnetic Poles

All magnets have ends called **poles**. These are the places on a magnet where the force is the strongest. One end is called the north pole. The other end is called the south pole.

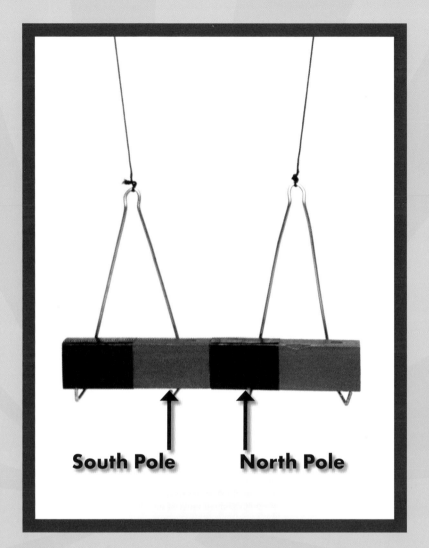

South Pole   **North Pole**

A pole on one magnet always pulls toward the opposite pole on another magnet.

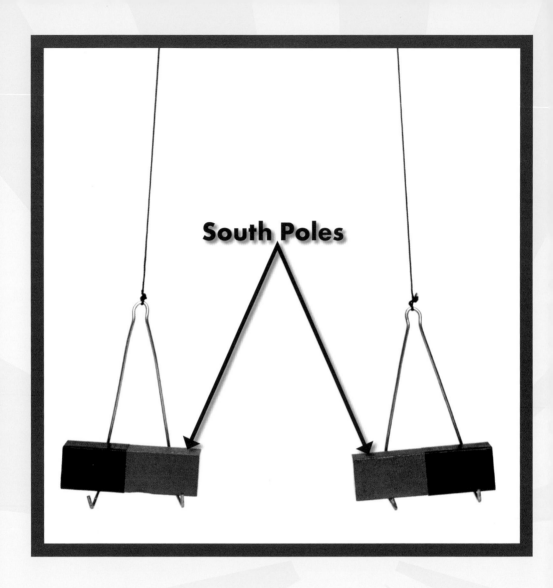

South Poles

Two of the same poles will always push away from each other. It is very difficult to hold the poles together. This pushing force is magnetism too.

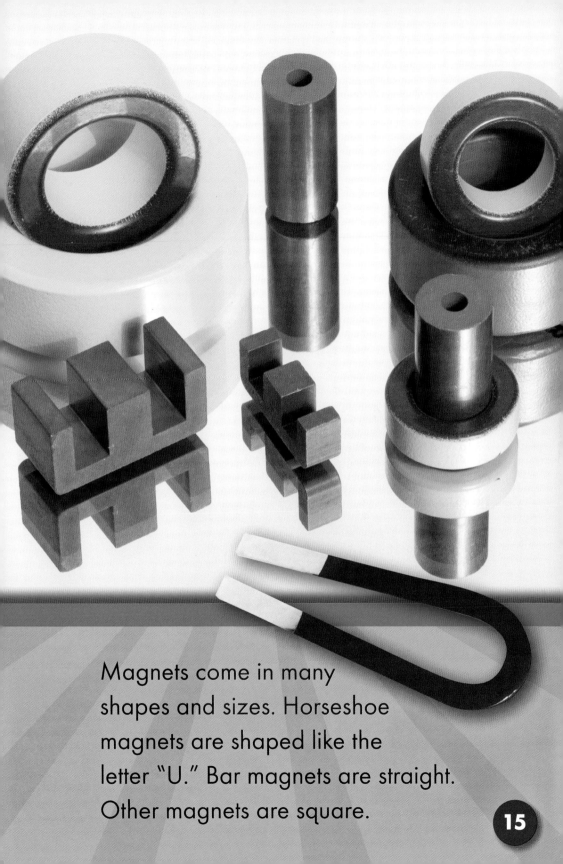

Magnets come in many shapes and sizes. Horseshoe magnets are shaped like the letter "U." Bar magnets are straight. Other magnets are square.

Magnetic Earth

Some magnets are really big. In fact, Earth is a huge magnet! Hot liquid metals deep inside Earth create magnetism. Like all magnets, Earth has two poles where magnetism is strongest. Earth's magnetic poles are near the **geographic** North and South Poles, but they are not the same points. The geographic poles mark the ends of Earth's **axis**, the imaginary line around which Earth rotates.

fun fact

The Earth's magnetic poles move over time. Scientists believe they move between 6 and 25 miles (10 and 40 kilometers) per year.

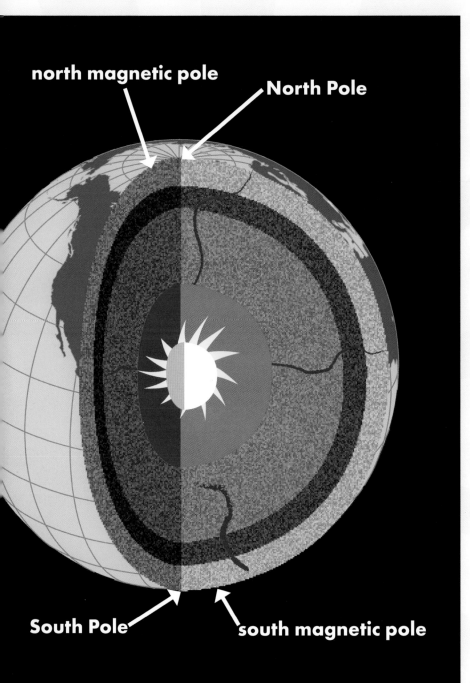

north magnetic pole

North Pole

South Pole

south magnetic pole

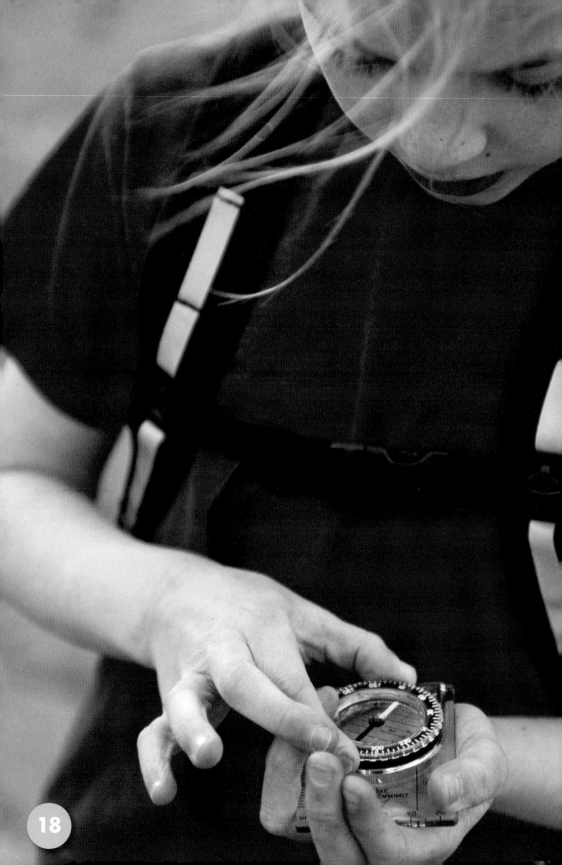

Earth's magnetic poles pull on smaller magnets. A **compass** is a tool with a magnetic needle. The needle is always pulled toward the north magnetic pole.

Have you ever been lost? A compass could help you find your way home. When you know which direction is north, you can figure out south, east, and west. Many people use compasses when they are hiking to help them find their way.

! fun fact

Animals don't need a compass to find their way like people do. Some animals, such as monarch butterflies and humpback whales, can sense Earth's magnetism. This ability helps them find their way when moving between their summer and winter homes.

Magnets in Use

Magnets are useful in many ways. Some trains use very strong magnets to move along their tracks. The pull of the magnets can make a train go very fast.

Magnetic brakes can also make the train stop. Are you ready for a ride on the magnetic express?

Glossary

aluminum—a metal found in nature that is not magnetic

axis—the imaginary line around which the earth rotates

compass—a tool with a magnetic needle that always points to magnetic north

copper—a reddish metal found in nature that is not magnetic

geographic—having to do with the earth's surface

iron—a metal found in nature that sticks to magnets

magnetic—being attracted to a magnet; magnetic metals include iron, steel, nickel, and cobalt.

pole—an end of a magnet; all magnets have two poles, a north pole and a south pole.

steel—a metal made from iron that sticks to magnets

To Learn More

AT THE LIBRARY

Cooper, Jason. *Magnets*. Vero Beach, Fla.: Rourke, 2003.

Morgan, Ben. *Magnetism*. San Diego, Calif.: Blackbirch Press, 2003.

Nelson, Robin. *Magnets*. Minneapolis, Minn.: Lerner Publications, 2004.

Olien, Becky. *Magnets*. Mankato, Minn.: Capstone Press, 2003.

Rosinsky, Natalie M. *Magnets: Pulling Together, Pushing Apart*. Minneapolis, Minn.: Picture Window Books, 2003.

ON THE WEB
Learning more about magnetism is as easy as 1, 2, 3.

1. Go to www.factsurfer.com

2. Enter "magnetism" into search box.

3. Click the "Surf" button and you will see a list of related web sites.

With factsurfer.com, finding more information is just a click away.

Index

aluminum, 9

animals, 19

axis, 16

compass, 19

copper, 9

directions, 19

Earth, 16, 17, 19

geographic poles, 16, 17

iron, 6

magnetic metals, 6, 16

magnetic poles, 12, 13, 14, 16, 17

non-magnetic metals, 9

refrigerator, 4, 7

steel, 6, 7, 10

trains, 20, 21

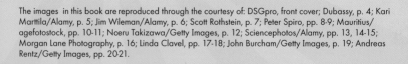

The images in this book are reproduced through the courtesy of: DSGpro, front cover; Dubassy, p. 4; Kari Marttila/Alamy, p. 5; Jim Wileman/Alamy, p. 6; Scott Rothstein, p. 7; Peter Spiro, pp. 8-9; Mauritius/agefotostock, pp. 10-11; Noeru Takizawa/Getty Images, p. 12; Sciencephotos/Alamy, pp. 13, 14-15; Morgan Lane Photography, p. 16; Linda Clavel, pp. 17-18; John Burcham/Getty Images, p. 19; Andreas Rentz/Getty Images, pp. 20-21.